P9-DGG-110

Animal
Homes

KINGFISHER

a Houghton Mifflin Company imprint
222 Berkeley Street
Boston, Massachusetts 02116
www.houghtonmifflinbooks.com

First published in 2003
2 4 6 8 10 9 7 5 3 1

1TR/0503/PROSP/RNB(RNB)/140MA

LIBRARY OF CONGRESS CATALOGING-IN-PUBLICATION DATA
has been applied for.

ISBN 0-7534-5616-8

Senior editor: Belinda Weber
Coordinating editor: Stephanie Pliakas
Designers: Sam Combes, Joanne Brown
Picture manager: Cee Weston-Baker
Illustrator: Steve Weston
DTP coordinator: Sarah Pfitzner
DTP operator: Primrose Burton
Artwork archivists: Wendy Allison, Jenny Lord
Senior production controller: Nancy Roberts
Indexer: Chris Bernstein

Printed in China

Acknowledgments
The Publisher would like to thank the following for permission to reproduce their material. Every care has been taken
to trace copyright holders. However, if there have been unintentional omissions or failure to trace copyright holders,
we apologize and will, if informed, endeavor to make corrections in any future edition.
b = bottom, *c* = center, *l* = left, *t* = top, *r* = right

Photographs: *cover*: Getty Images; 4-5 National Geographic Image Collection; 8 Oxford Scientific Films (OSF); 9*t* OSF; 9*b* OSF;
10 OSF; 11*t* Getty Images; 11*b* OSF; 12-13 Getty Images; 13*c* Corbis; 14 Corbis; 15*t* Corbis; 15*b* Corbis; 16 Nature Picture Library;
18*tl* Nature Picture Library; 18-19 National Geographic Image Collection; 19*t* Getty Images; 21 Ardea; 22*tr* Nature Picture Library;
22*b* Natural History Picture Agency (NHPA); 23*t* Corbis; 23*b* Nature Picture Library; 26 Corbis; 27 Ardea; 28-29 National Geographic
Image Collection; 29*t* Corbis; 30*bl* OSF; 31*t* Corbis; 31*b* Ardea; 32*t* NHPA; 32-33 NHPA; 33*b* NHPA; 35*t* NHPA; 36 Corbis;
36-37 Still Pictures; 37 OSF; 38 Corbis; 38-39 Getty Images; 39 Nature Picture Library

Commissioned photography on pages 42–47 by Andy Crawford.
Thank you to models Eleanor Davis, Lewis Manu, Daniel Newton, Lucy Newton, Nikolas Omilana, and Olivia Omilana.

Kingfisher Young Knowledge

Animal Homes

Angela Wilkes

KINGFISHER

BOSTON

Contents

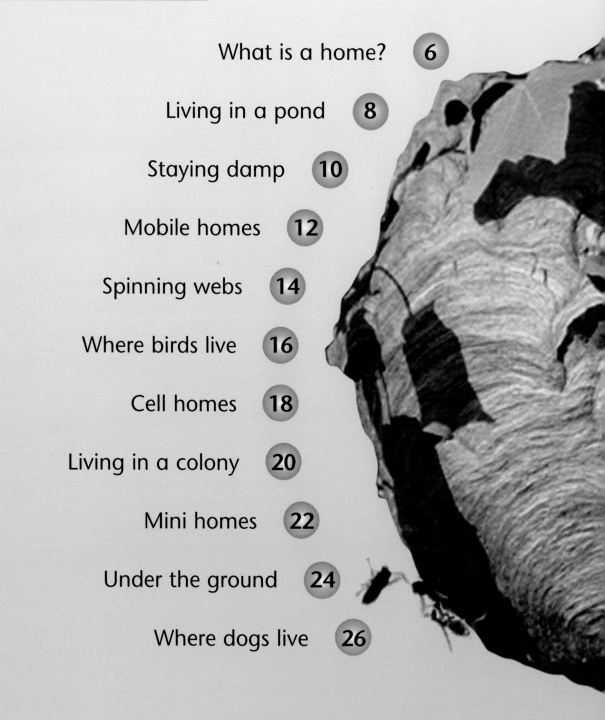

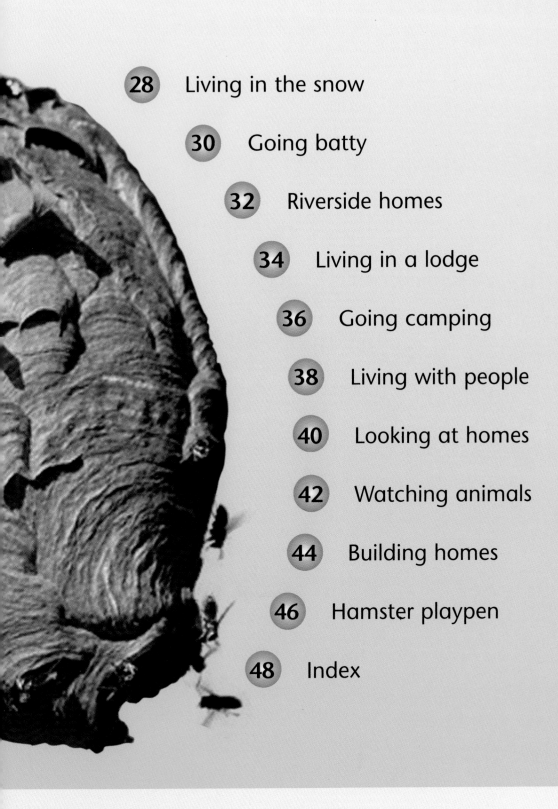

What is a home?

Animals need homes for all of the same reasons that people do. Homes provide shelter and keep animals warm in the winter. They are a safe place to rest and to raise babies.

Hard to find

Animals build their homes out of materials that match their surroundings. This makes it hard for predators to spot them.

predators—animals that hunt and eat other animals

Safe place for babies

Homes, such as this bird's nest, are only built to raise babies. A nest is warm, cozy, and away from danger. This is where a mother bird lays her eggs and raises her young.

Different homes

Animals build many types of homes. Some build nests, while others make dens or dig burrows.

Living in a pond

Many different animals live in the still, freshwater of a pond. Here they can find good hiding places and many things to eat.

Finding a mate

Newts live in ponds in the spring. They look for a mate and then lay their eggs in the water.

Blowing bubbles

The water spider spins a web between water plants. It then fills its web with air to make a bubble in which it can live.

Fatherly love

A male stickleback sticks plants together to make a nest. A female lays her eggs in the nest, and the male fans freshwater over them with his fins.

Staying damp

Amphibians, such as frogs and toads, live in damp, shady places. They need to keep their skin moist and slimy. Some build their homes in unusual spots.

Living in a hole

When it rains, the water-holding frog's skin soaks up water. The slime on its skin sets to make a cocoon that keeps in the water. The frog then burrows into the sand to escape from the desert heat.

water-holding frog

amphibian—*animal that is born in water but then lives on land*

Treetop homes

Strawberry poison
dart frogs live in
steamy rain forests.
They hide from the
hot sun in pools
of rainwater that
collect in between
huge plants.

Burrowing toads

Spadefoot toads dig burrows
and spend most of their time there.
But when it rains, they go above
ground to find mates.

cocoon—wrapping that protects an animal

Mobile homes

Some animals live in a shell that they carry on their backs. The hard shell shields the animal's soft body from knocks and bumps and shelters it from the wind and rain. It also protects it from hungry predators that are looking for food.

Suit of armor

A tortoise has a tough shell shaped like a dome. If the tortoise is in danger, it pulls its head and legs back into its shell.

shield—to protect and take care of

A home that grows

As a snail grows its shell grows too—so the shell is always just the right size. Snails slink back inside their shells to hide from danger.

Borrowed home

A hermit crab has no hard shell of its own, so it finds an empty mollusk shell and moves in. When it grows, the hermit crab moves to a bigger shell.

mollusk—an animal with a soft body and a hard shell

Spinning webs

Most spiders spin webs in order to catch insects. They build them using silk threads from their own bodies. But some spiders live in other types of homes such as holes or burrows.

Cobweb trap

The orb spider spins a beautiful sticky web between the stems of plants. The spider waits for insects in the center of the web or hides under a nearby leaf.

prey—*an animal that is hunted and killed by another animal*

Under a rock

Some spiders make nests in hollow spaces under rocks. They line the nest with thick silk and lay their eggs. Then they wait to pounce on passing insects.

Surprise attack!

The trap-door spider digs a tunnel and lines it with silk. Then it makes a lid on top like a trapdoor. The spider hides in the tunnel and darts out to catch prey.

Where birds live

Birds build nests so that they have a warm, safe place to lay their eggs and raise their chicks. Most birds' nests are in trees, but some are on steep cliffs or even on the ground.

Hanging nest

The penduline tit hangs its purse-shaped nest from a twig. It is lined with soft wool and fluff from reeds or catkins to make a cozy home for the female and babies.

catkin—a spike of small, soft flowers on a tree

Fancy work

A male cape weaverbird weaves a complicated oval nest using grass and reeds. The only entrance is through a short tunnel at the bottom. This helps protect it from predators.

Hungry chicks

Chicks hatch in their nest. They are helpless and cannot leave. They open their beaks wide to beg for food.

*wasp larva
in a cell*

Cell homes

Wasps and bees
build amazing nests
that are made up of
many tiny cells. Young
wasps and bees can
grow up safely in these
little compartments.

Laying eggs

A queen wasp lays
one egg in each cell.
Each egg will become
a wasp larva. Older
wasps take care of
the eggs and larvae.

Paper home

A wasp's nest is
made of layers of paper
wrapped around the larvae
cells. The wasps make paper
by chewing up wood and
mixing it with their saliva.

larva—a young insect that has just come out of its egg

Moving around 19

Bees live and work together. When bees need a new home, they fly away in a huge group called a swarm.

Honeycomb homes

Bees' nests are called hives. Inside a hive are wax honeycombs made up of many cells. The cells hold honey or baby bees.

larvae—*more than one larva*

leafcutter ants

Living in a colony

Most ants and termites live in huge groups called colonies. They work together to build enormous nests where they can raise their young.

Food for the colony

Leafcutter ants live in rain forests. They bite off pieces of leaves and carry them back to their nest. They store the leaves in special gardens, where a fungus grows on them, making a tasty food for the ants.

queen termite

***fungus**—a plant, such as a mushroom, that grows on other plants*

food
supplies

nursery
galleries

Leafy nest

All of the weaver ants work together to make their home—even the larvae! The young make a special sticky thread that the ants use to stick leaves together. The finished nest looks like a big leafy ball.

Mud castle

Termites build a giant dirt mound above their nest to keep it cool. Inside are nursery galleries for the young, as well as spaces for the queen and food supplies.

galleries—long rooms or passages

Mini homes

Mice live in many different places. Some live in fields, and some live in forests. Others even live in people's houses. But all mice build nests to rest in and to raise their babies.

Close to people

House mice make their nests using shredded paper, old rags, or grass. They always build their nests in a small hiding place that is out of sight.

shredded—torn into strips

Grassy homes

The tiny harvest mouse lives in tall grass. It weaves strips of grass around plant stems in order to make a cozy, round nest.

Sleepy mouse

In the fall the dormouse makes a cozy nest using shredded bark. Then it curls up into a ball and goes to sleep for the long, cold winter.

bark—*the outer layer of a tree's trunk or branches*

Under the ground

Marmots live high up in the mountains. When the first winter snows fall, the whole family moves into a big burrow lined with grass and goes to sleep.

Fast asleep

Marmots block the entrance to their burrow with rocks and soil to stop predators from getting in. Then they snuggle together to stay warm and hibernate until the spring returns.

hibernate—*to spend the whole winter in a deep sleep*

Where dogs live

Foxes and dingoes are wild dogs. They build their homes by digging dens in soft dirt or by taking over and enlarging the homes of other animals. Dens provide shelter from the hot sun or cold weather and are a safe place to raise pups.

Desert homes
Kit foxes live in stony deserts in North America. They sleep in their dens during the day when it is most hot. At night, when it is cooler, they go out hunting.

den—a sheltered place where an animal lives

Ready-made den

Dingoes live in Australia. When a mother dingo is about to have pups, she moves into a safe den. This is often a big hole underneath tree roots or some rocks.

enlarging—making bigger

28 Living in the snow

Polar bears live in the snowy Arctic. When they are tired, they dig a shallow pit in the snow and sleep in it. In the fall a pregnant polar bear digs a den in a snowdrift. This is where she will spend the long, dark winter.

Snow babies

The mother bear stays in the den until the spring. In the early winter she gives birth to one or two cubs. She feeds them her milk, and they all sleep for most of the winter.

pregnant—going to have a baby

Leaving the den

In the spring the polar
bear and her young come
out of the den. The mother
is very hungry since she has
not eaten all winter long.
She takes her cubs
onto the sea ice,
where she
can hunt
for food.

sea ice—*ice that forms on the surface of the sea when it freezes*

Going batty

Bats hunt for food at night and rest during the day. They do not make special homes but instead roost in trees, caves, barns, or even attics.

Leafy shelter

Fruit bats live in huge groups called colonies and roost in tall trees during the day. They hang upside down from branches, clinging on tightly with the claws on their feet. Then they wrap their skinny wings around themselves for protection.

roost—to settle down to sleep

Dark caves

Many bats sleep in large caves.
Thousands of them roost upside
down, packed closely together.
At night the bats set out to
feed. Some bats eat insects.
Others, like these fruit
bats, eat fruit and the
nectar from flowers.

Riverside homes

dragonfly

Many animals live on the banks of rivers and streams. There they are close to freshwater, and there are enough plants, small creatures, and fish to eat. They are also safely out of reach of most predators.

Water babies

Adult dragonflies live beside rivers. The larvae live in the water. When the larvae are ready to become adults, they climb up a plant's stem. Their skin splits open along their backs, and the adult dragonflies climb out.

Nest tunnel

Kingfishers dig tunnels in a soft riverbank. At the end of the tunnel the female kingfisher makes a small chamber and lays her eggs. When the chicks hatch, she brings them fish to eat.

Rest burrows

Platypuses live close to lakes and rivers. A mother platypus digs a long, nesting burrow in the bank's soft dirt. There she lays her eggs and raises her babies.

chamber—a room

Living in a lodge

Beavers are smart builders. They construct dams across streams in order to make ponds. Then they build homes, called lodges, in the middle of these ponds.

Safe from enemies

The beavers line the lodge with dry grasses to keep it snug and warm. All of the entrances are underwater, safe from predators.

Timber!

Using their sharp front teeth, beavers can cut down trees. They gnaw around the bottom of a tree until it falls down. Then they chew pieces off to make small logs.

Saving food for later

Beavers only eat plants. They store some food at the bottom of the pond so they can eat all winter long.

Going camping

Big apes, such as chimpanzees, orangutans, and gorillas, do not have one home. Instead they move from place to place. At night they make leafy nests and camp out.

Climbing trees

Chimpanzees make tree nests at nighttime. They bend leafy branches to make comfortable beds where they can sleep.

ape—*an animal that looks like a monkey without a tail*

Leafy nests

Orangutans build two tree nests each day. They build a small nest for a nap. At night they build platforms in the forks of trees.

Heavy sleepers

Female gorillas nest in trees. Male gorillas build nests on the ground since they are too heavy to sleep in trees!

Living with people

Towns and cities provide shelter, food, and warmth. As these places have gotten bigger, more animals have moved into them. Animals often settle into new homes in the most surprising places.

Cardboard bed

In North America raccoons have moved to town gardens and even into city centers. They live in attics and sheds. Raccoons eat almost anything and even help themselves to food from garbage cans.

platform—*a flat surface*

Living the high life

The peregrine falcon usually lives on cliff or rock faces. In cities it roosts on churches, tall buildings, and even on radio antennae.

Chimney homes

For hundreds of years the white stork has nested close to people. It builds its huge nest on top of chimneys and houses. Some people build special platforms for storks to nest on.

40 Looking at homes

You will need
- Plastic cup
- Scissors
- Plastic food wrap
- Rubber bands

Make a pond viewer
With this simple underwater viewer you can take a closer look at the small creatures that live in ponds and streams.

Hold the plastic cup firmly in one hand. Then hold the scissors in your other hand and carefully cut out the bottom of the cup.

Cut out a large circle of plastic food wrap. Stretch it tightly over the cut end of the cup until the plastic wrap is smooth.

Stretch a few rubber bands over the plastic wrap to hold it in place. Pull the edges of the plastic wrap tight again.

To use the pond viewer dip the end covered with plastic wrap into the water. Then look through the open end at the top of the cup.

Make a nest

Watch different birds making their nests in the spring. See if you can copy them by making a bird's nest of your own.

You will need
- Paintbrush and glue
- Plastic bowl
- Dried grass
- Moss
- Feathers and leaves
- Candy wrappers

Using a paintbrush, spread glue all around the outside of the bowl. Pick up small handfuls of dried grass and stick them onto the bowl.

Spread glue around the inside of the bowl. Then stick on a layer of more dried grass and moss in order to make a soft, cozy center.

Scatter a few small feathers and leaves inside the nest to make it look realistic. Decorate with a few candy wrappers to add color.

42 Watching animals

Make a tepee hideout

If you make a simple tepee in your yard or local park,
you can hide inside it and watch animals.

You will need

- Large white sheet
- 4 bamboo canes
- Garden twine
- Paintbrush
- Scissors
- Poster paints

1 Mix the paints with some water
so they are easy to use. Paint
circles and other bold shapes on
the sheet. Leave the sheet to dry.

2 Stand the four bamboo
canes together and make
them into a tepee shape.
Cut a long piece of twine
and tie the canes together
firmly at the top.

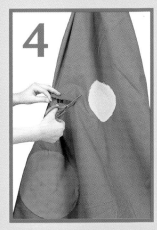

Wrap the sheet around the tepee frame. Tie it in place at the top of the canes using more twine.

See where your face comes up to on the sheet. Cut out a peephole big enough for you to see out.

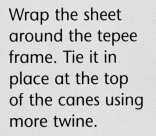

Go inside the tepee hideout and close the loose edges of the sheet behind you. Stay as quiet and still as you can and wait to see which animals come close. Take a notebook and pencil so you can take notes about what you see.

44 Building homes

Make a hermit crab

Make a crab out of modeling clay and put it in an empty shell. Then it will be just like a real hermit crab!

You will need
- Shell
- Modeling clay
- Pipe cleaner

Roll two pieces of modeling clay into balls for the crab's head and body. Make four small sausage shapes for the legs and some claw shapes.

Break off two tiny pieces of a different color modeling clay. Roll them into little balls for the eyes and stick them onto the head.

Attach the head, claws, and legs to the crab's body. Make feelers from two pieces of pipe cleaner and then put the crab in the shell.

Flowerpot home
Make a flowerpot home for insects. Check to see what is inside it every day and draw the creatures you find there.

You will need
- Flowerpot
- Small rock
- Notebook and pen

Ask an adult to help you find a shady spot somewhere near your house. Turn the flowerpot upside down and prop it up on the rock.

After a few days look inside the flowerpot. Draw pictures in your notebook of any creatures you find. Can you name them?

Bee home
Make this simple bee box and hang it in a sunny place outside. The straws should slope down into the bottle.

You will need
- Large plastic bottle
- Drinking straws
- Scissors
- String

Cut off the top end off the bottle and fill it with straws. Then tie string around the bottle and hang it outside.

46 Hamster playpen

Build a playpen

Your pet hamster or mouse will have a lot of fun with this playpen. It can climb in and out of it, as if on a jungle gym.

You will need
- Shoe box
- 4 empty toilet paper rolls
- Poster paints
- Scissors
- Paintbrush
- Pencil
- Plastic cup

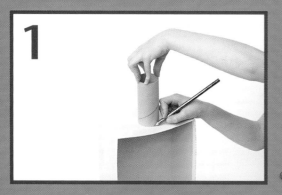

Position a toilet roll in the middle of one end of the shoe box and trace around it. Repeat on the other sides of the box.

Make a hole in the center of one circle and cut out lines to the edge of it. Then cut out the circle. Do this with all of the circles on the box.

Mix some poster paint with some water in a plastic cup and carefully paint the shoe box. Then leave the box to dry.

4

5

Paint the cardboard tubes a different color. Paint one half of each tube and let it dry. Then paint the other half of the tube and leave that to dry as well.

Push the cardboard tubes into the holes around the sides of the box. They should fit firmly and stick out a bit. Now see if your hamster wants to play!

Index